THE FIRE IN ALL THINGS

THE FIRE IN ALL THINGS

poems by STEPHEN YENSER

LOUISIANA STATE UNIVERSITY PRESS
Baton Rouge and London

Designer: Glynnis Phoebe
Typeface: Bembo
Typesetter: G&S Typesetters, Inc.
Printer and binder: Thomson-Shore, Inc.

Library of Congress Cataloging-in-Publication Data

Yenser, Stephen.
    The fire in all things : poems / by Stephen Yenser.
        p.   cm.
    ISBN 0-8071-1827-3.—ISBN 0-8071-1828-1 (pbk.)
    I. Title.
    PS3575.E53F57   1993
    811'.54—dc20   92-2457
                                              CIP

The poems listed have been published previously, often in different versions, in the following publications: *Canto*, "Nulla Dies Sine Linea," "Pentimento," "Reconnaissance," "Woodcut"; *Creative Arts*, "Counterparts" (as "Bilingual"); *Massachusetts Review*, "Grounds" (as "Premises"), "Terminal Moraine," *"Makila,"* "Another Term," "On the Block," "New Leaves," "Eaux Bonnes," "Old Haunts"; *Nation*, "Fundamental"; *Paris Review*, "Art History," "Voices," "Carnal Knowledge"; *Partisan Review*, "A Table of Greene Fields"; *Poetry*, "Intensive Care," "The Racket," "Moving Again," "Common Property"; *Poetry Northwest*, "Equinox," "Transhumance" (as "Equinox"); *Southwest Review*, "Sentence"; *Westwind*, "Homecoming at Lammas"; *Yale Review*, "Ember Week, Reseda," "Vertumnal." "Notebook Entry" first appeared in the March 14, 1977, issue of *The New Yorker*. "Paros" first appeared in *For James Merrill: A Birthday Tribute* (Jordan Davies, 1986) and then as a chapbook published by Jordan Davies the same year. A shorter version of "Clos Camardon" was published as a chapbook by Sea Cliff Press in 1985.

Publication of this book has been supported by a grant from the National Endowment for the Arts in Washington, D.C., a federal agency.

The paper in this book meets the guidelines for permanence and durability of the Committee on Production Guidelines for Book Longevity of the Council on Library Resources.∞

To Melissa Berton

Μήτε μοὶ μέλι, μήτε μέλισσα.

CONTENTS

I

FUNDAMENTAL

Loam. Jasmine. Honeysuckle. The rain has fallen
Silent, and now the silence too is dead.

Night crawlers turn through it and snuggle up
Close for comfort.

This is the time to call a spade,
A shade, a heart transmuted

To an instrument then laid aside
And multiplied upon a vine. Old tutor,

High climber, help me put down raveled roots
And take up ramifying things:

Ground-breaking, path-breaking, breaking
In, out, up—anyway, I need you now.

And you, sweet friend, night bloomer, show me how
Not to stop

Yet, how to pluck, to be plucked like the harp
The rain has hanged upon the willow

Before it learns the plot to break
What even now its moonwashed gold bespeaks

And calls the author of the thunder
Down like dawn upon the thief's bowed head.

CLOS CAMARDON

"The story is not ended," said that glum, spike-chinned cleric.

The king moved with jovial impatience.

"If you continue it," he said, "it will surely come to an end sometime. A stone on a stone makes a house, dear heart, and a word on a word tells a tale."

—James Stephens, "The Wooing of Becfola"

GROUNDS

Well, that's an end of that.
And houses really do fall down—
At least they do in that province
Where they are rarely pulled down
Before they've had a chance
To give in to the tremors, freezes, vines.

The old Clos out behind was falling down,
So we were told by our landlady
Through whose blue-filtered, unfilmed time exposures
We saw the villa with its vanished vineyard,
Whose last first-place award
Under September's thunderstorms fast fades

Its true blue streak, its shades of *lie-de-vin,*
Shades of your last year's new maquillage,
Down its namesake's whitewash . . .
Enough. Back here the winds come up,
Hoping to have some caution thrown to them,
Now silence has been broken like a camp.

NULLA DIES SINE LINEA

Fall evenings in Béarn the sunlight fell
Through streaky panes the parlor's worn Bokhara
Translated on the spot to rich stained glass.
We'd drink to that day's work, the watered wine
The wash's color in that aquarelle
I'd titled for you. By then you'd turned to oils,

Turned to others. Meanwhile I had my own
Torch to carry—as did the new oil well
On the nearest hill. From my desk window
Two stories up, I'd watch the flaming gas
Whip in the wind, a manic sable brush
Burning to top that cypress in Van Gogh,

To be a candle held to Valéry . . .
But there were moments even I could see
How both ends burned. "Le chagrin de Pau,"
I thought to call one gloomy villanelle.
You smiled at that. Then we went brightly on
Talking and painting out the night.

TERMINAL MORAINE

Stones that the glacier had dug up,
Ground out, begrudged, but then bequeathed
(Even that mother of all hunks of ice
Was polished off at last),
Heaved in wheelbarrows or just lugged by hand
Both to clear the fields and to build up

The old Clos's walls on which the joists and ties
Bore their weight until they rotted,
Long after they had gone,
Those owners who could do their own repairing:
These now mark paths where you did time
For whom the marriage was a hill

Up which you hauled a stone
You found lackluster, awkward, hard to slip
As your philosopher's to understand,
A code to break—and yet you must have known
We would get to the bottom of it all
Too soon without my help.

NOTEBOOK ENTRY

Oh yes, that week . . . Remember how one day,
Late for class, as usual too slow
Then fast, I jarred the gatepost from its socket,
Upsetting too both you and our landlady?
For days I tried to coax and rock
It back into its secret place,

But no amount of pressure, no lever worked.
Like that poem where things would not click,
The one that, tipsy, angry, looking
For ways to get to me through my thick notebook,
You'd come upon a clumsy fragment of
("Bored stiff by his own horny verse he'd head

Off to find her stiff as a board in bed"),
In fact like you when you had read it, love,
It was stubbornly unhinged.
So in the end we paid to have it done.
It took a local handyman a half
Hour or less. Ah, how one had to laugh.

MAKILA

"Walking stick." Sparks jumped
From where one steel point struck the stone
The afternoons you'd followed
A friend and two half-jackal hounds
Past the clearing down into the woods
And I would strike out through them on my own

Toward town. The other point, a goad,
Fit in the grip I couldn't seem to keep
Screwed on the shaft of sculpted medlar,
Slit on the living branch, then cauterized,
And then cut down to size and shape,
The warped straightforwardness we prized.

Makila. The only Basque we learned
Brings back woods hanging fire at our arrival,
Brings you up from them later in the year,
When they had turned bare birch and ash.
But there's no point today, since you have turned
Away for good, in all this striking out.

RECONNAISSANCE

This life . . . you will have to live once more and
innumerable times more . . . and everything . . . must
return to you—all in the same succession and sequence.
—Nietzsche's demon

And so the same streetwalkers down in Pau
Will once more do a bang-up business all
That night. I'll scout them in our old Renault,
Camouflage green and rusty, still undented,
Shaped like a German army helmet—in search, I guess,
Of someone to surrender to.

The next day war will be resumed. Once more
We'll find ourselves in those two hornets bombed
Out of their minds there on the windowsill.
Grounded, dying to get at one another,
They'll writhe and sizzle, fizzling out at last
Like fractured Chinese firecrackers.

But one time, too, out of the midnight blue,
Just as it happened then, if Nietzsche's right,
A crackling silence must end in our bed,
Where later you will touch my lips and laugh,
Then whisper, "Well, you might not talk enough,
Mais tu as la langue bien pendue."

ANOTHER TERM

It's later there than here. It always was.
And even colder. You'll have lit your heater—
And I have just remembered the *mazout*
My fingers smelled of, bitter winter nights,
Derives from distillation from raw gas
Of that much dearer fuel, plain old *essence,*

Its name from Arabic, whose soft coughs we'd practiced
In Baghdad's souks. The residue was so
Slow to ignite, I poured pure spirits on,
Then flipped a match, from a certain distance. Tonight,
The moment strikes its match, flames leap to catch
Our breath, back in that other room and country . . .

But those are flames one has committed since
To memory, along with grimmer scenes
One keeps committing in cold blood,
All those to which one must someday,
For better and for worse, and even if
No home's a certain cure, commit oneself.

SENTENCE

"If Nietzsche's right recurrence is eternal"—
And every aeon I'll sit here and pore
Coldly as moonlight over this bleak journal.
You'd think the grim rehashing that's internal
Would be enough. But I've said *that* before,
If Nietzsche's right. Recurrence is eternal

And exact. It's not just this hibernal
Landscape but each snowflake time must restore.
So I'll have preread this ringbound journal
In which I'll set down those intense nocturnal
Remissions that the next day we'd deplore . . .
If Nietzsche's right, recurrence is; eternal

Returns are earned. The homeless earn infernal
Fires in steel drums; the rich, each warm encore.
So which are we? The sentence in this journal,
Whose pages show that some cast out the kernel
And chew the husk, will never tell us more:
"If Nietzsche's right recurrence is eternal."

ON THE BLOCK

That is why if we are unwilling to die we cannot make
anything that will live; writer's block is an attempt
to put off the death that would leave something behind,
as our faith in "creativity" reflects the wish to
continue forever in a state of permanent life without death.
— Jonathan Bishop, *Something Else*

Me with my faithful phrase books
(*Toujours aux basques de quelqu'un*),
Me with my missing pieces, my commonplace
Building blocks
(*Il n'y a que le premier pas qui coûte*),
Hunched at the desk, hot, cold, stiff, mute

(Steady heat was what the cat was in),
Fighting off the next day's lecture,
And you off in your studio—
Slaves both, in our own separate ways,
As strugglebound as Michelangelo's.
"Chiseling passion of its pound of flesh,"

I started one more thing I couldn't finish.
I put it by, when you two hit the hay
(*N'éveillez pas le chat qui dort*),
To "rate the cost of the erection"
(*Henry IV*). Love, love—a little *mort*,
They used to say, was going all the way.

NEW LEAVES

Wagtails cut in and out
Of ash and birch that meant to mend their ways
Above all else, while down to earth
Half-buried stones lay still and grew their moss.
Saplings rose to greet us by the hearth,
And vines redid the walls, both in and out,

Struggling to leave no precious stone unturned.
Terrific tug-of-war? Or hug of life?
The evening light declined to illuminate
Just what the ruin meant to us,
That every blessèd day
We had to keep on going to it.

It took some months.
And it took more than some—well, gall,
To think that I could write you off.
Yet I can hardly thank you
For leaving me
Enough.

EQUINOX

With chirps of crickets, squeaks
Of unoiled shutter hinges
And pulleys dropping buckets
Back down black wells, the spring uncoiled
At last, and that year's ice was broken
In roadside streams in villages

Where *les croulantes* survive to gossip
And each house takes its turn
Doing its lingerie in public.
Up in your mountains, every year,
Each gorge divulges its own informations,
However muddled or crystal clear,

However chilling, and then before one knows it,
In less time than the stern grandfather clock
Measured with weight and chain
Until it too ran out,
If just to get rewound again,
The vine has wrapped the winter's story up.

EAUX BONNES

Eight months, to be exact,
The mistletoe on each old oak
Advanced your argument: roots tie one down.
No matter how I chopped its logic
Made twisted sense. You cried, you packed
Off up the valley, wired back from Eaux Bonnes,

It rained, the water over it washed out
The dam next month—and our last year was gone.
Well. It was academic anyway.
Tonight's wire's broken words would cross an ocean.
There is no going back so far,
So far there's been no going forward. Yet

Whatever comes up next
(Remember how one morning you drove down
To the Atlantic there to watch sunrise,
Only to have it dawn on you . . . ?)
Will be the sun, another burning bridge,
A means of shedding light on some new text.

TRANSHUMANCE

April mornings I slogged out and back
In a dead man's rubber boots
Our widowed friend dug up for me.
On the run-down heels, and in the filling steps
Of winter dying in their tracks,
The dye-marked sheep came through. Along the lanes

They left, long johns and counterpanes
Flapped and sheets snapped whitely in an air
Too fresh to be summery,
Too laced with salt and balsam not to be.
And it was suddenly so clear so far
That even peak and cirque,

The glacier's own retreats,
Well beyond the last resort,
Could not keep their misty distance . . .
Damn it, Lorna, the days grew longer and longer
That draw in now. They too can hardly stand
Still for your departure.

WOODCUT

Along our woods' main path vines gripped
The trees as tightly as barbed wire, but thick.
The largest one that I could find to chop
Was thick as my wrist,
Close as a bulging vein along the trunk.
Chopped short, its stem rose from beneath the root

Of one fine oak (the one whose lopped off limb
Had left a scar you thought so labial),
Like a serpent stiff with pain beneath its foot.
There's some hard emblem there of our hard spring,
Its edifying motto lost, ripped
Out with the vine's own binding script.

First days back here, lights going slowly out
Out in the lemon trees, I'd start to write
To you, then get a grip upon myself,
Sharpen several pencils, date a page.
The stars turned on above. This way and that,
Love goes on grinding on its axes.

PENTIMENTO

Courbet painted out of "L'Atelier,"
At an angry Baudelaire's request, the latter's
Wicked black orchid, the banished Jeanne Duval.
You'd taken me to see it in the Louvre,
Showed me where through the years, through the impasto
Hiding her, she has returned at last,

Meanwhile slipping into something more
Subdued, if nonetheless extraordinary.
For there she floats, as though on glass, a ghost
The poet hasn't noticed, having lost
Himself by now in some illegible
Volume he's reading, perched on a table's edge.

Not quite there at his shoulder, eldritch, elfin,
She looks beyond him either for the self
Still sunken in the dark depths of the mirror
Behind him or, in the mirror, at her
Laughable lover reading. Poe? Balzac?
No matter. One day soon he'll want her back.

DOMESTIC

Leaf-cutting bees, at work on winter nests,
Were turning lilac leaves to bobbin lace
Along the path, cobbled with chestnut burs,
Below your studio. I'd take a leaf,
Sometimes, or stuff my jacket pockets full.
Inside the prickly shells, as snug as lovers,

Lay pairs of nuts—each lustrous as the briar
The old Basque shepherd polished on his nose
The day we sat, backs to the ancient wall
Above Saint-Jean-Pied-de-Port, and laughed
At scurrilous local tales. On each façade,
In place of an address, there was a date:

1601, 1828 . . .
Estrangements, adulteries,
Revenge—old chestnuts, Stephen. Let them lie,
Please. Or end up like those aging bees
Fabre wrote about, that couldn't stop
Sealing off deserted galleries.

OLD HAUNTS

The silver birch will have been turned
To gold by now, the bracken,
As though in someone's memory already,
Like the Chantilly that our landlady found
Packed in her trunk once its lock had been broken,
A crepitant gold leaf.

The day I left there, at the end of summer,
Out in the Clos one birch leaf turned and turned
In pirouette, in midair, at the end,
Most likely, of a gossamer.
If not dear life, dear heart, what else,
And for what could it have been hanging on?

Surely no words of mine. And you'd long gone.
And now—but then, *pas seul, pas seul*: same thing.
One's bound to find the way to lose oneself.
I did. I do. By that clerestory light,
Motes thick as pollen in it, where the trees
Arch above the path we'd always taken.

EMBER WEEK, RESEDA

Back here the fall, spreading down the hills,
Scatters its seeds of fire through mountain ash
And gingko, the occasional pistache,
The sour gum and the purple plum alike.
Here and there a liquidambar burns
Wickedly as it turns

Its deep flame up. The fire in all things loves
The end of them. Underfoot the leaves
Crackle like crumpled letters. Even the rain,
Dripping its last at midnight from the eaves,
Pops and snaps out on the front porch steps.
Watching the logs give in

And glow, the fire like memory revise
Those other windblown trees' slow-motion blaze,
Your brush lick at a glaze of crimson lake
Somewhere in the dreamlike, liquid world
The heat's a window on, I catch myself
Again, falling awake.

II

COMMON PROPERTY

To hell with it. Two long-planned trips
Deferred, and four full months on one brief sequence,
About that other trip, which changed us so,
And I am *still* as cold and hard to start
Each day as my bête noire, the Quatre Chevaux
Of our apocalypse.

I'm stuck at home again. A fuggy flat.
And when I open windows things
With sharp details zing back and forth and out
And in as though I were myself that house
I couldn't write from, meant to write about,
And they the bees that built in it.

But first there were the swallows—
Although I didn't know till late
In that French winter our fair-weather friends
Were what had fouled the flue, reduced the heat.
One morning, shoveling out the clinker,
I found what seemed at first the mate

Of our half-molten weathercock,
The "chimney piece" we'd picked up on a walk
With John up to the ruin on the rise,
The house gone up in smoke years back.
Now one would think real birds too wise
To be attached to such a spot,

Would think that instinct would have taught
That smothered fires could do them in . . .
Yet even birds of a feather,
It seemed to us when we had talked,
Must know more than to stick together
Through such a literal thick and thin.

And sure enough: the chimney's sconce
Only held a blackened nest. You shrugged:
"One swallow didn't make the winter."
We did, somehow, and so the bees would suffer,
When they returned that spring to their old haunts,
Stick upon acrid stick of burning sulphur.

Every morning workers would succumb
And tumble inside laden with their honey,
Which then was dutifully collected
By desperate survivors. It's funny—
They wanted to leave the awful nest they'd stirred,
Yet strangely couldn't. A timid queen,

Or hatching plans, or something kept them there.
One day, up on the roof, they swarmed
At last, a tiny, manic storm—
And then, as the real thing came up,
Beside themselves with indecision,
Inched back over the chimney's lip.

All afternoon we lived in that dark din
Of rain and sweet frustration.
For once you couldn't hike off with your friend.
Next morning, buzzing around the house,
They looked as though they meant
To wrap the whole thing up.

Your turn came first. The day I drove
Back through the hairpin curves,
Having helped you move
Closer to nature and to better lovers
Of it than I, I glanced into the mirror
To see flames leaping through the back lid's louvers.

Of course there was that stream,
A farmer with a bucket. Smoke and steam.
A cut. Some stitches. Then one final row.
According to the marriage settlement,
The scorched but salvaged body's yours.
That's fine. I couldn't move it anyhow.

ART HISTORY

Either happiness or art. On doit trouver le bonheur dans son art. [The great artists'] lives have become atrophied, like an organ they no longer use.
—Rilke to Clara Westhoff, 5 September 1902

In front of Notre Dame, shy and sly,
With an awkward, a kind of duckward walk,
The young *clochard* edged up to women tourists
So occupied with their blue guides and green
They hardly noticed he was holding something
Next to him, down low, so gingerly,
In both his hands, we thought it could be injured.
Given a sudden glimpse, they'd flutter off
And then resettle, ignoring him. That evening,
Years back, your great, your undone work before you
Still, in that Champs café, flushed from Pernod,
Breasts pushed up by your thick, tanned, sculptor's wrist
Resting on the blue-veined marble table,
You talked about the nave, the rebuilt spire,
The Virgin with her foot upon the serpent
(Restored), and not the animated gargoyle
Who'd picked you out, much as a boy would choose
A favorite girl to frighten with his toad.
And yet: what were you thinking, as we drifted back—
What did you see most clearly, in your mind's eye,
That dark within suffused as by a light
Subtler and warmer than the great rose window's?
But how to keep these things apart, you muse
From somewhere far. *The flèche, for instance,* its hard
Imperative, *and his bared soul itself,*
Unwrinkling, growing guileless once again.

COUNTERPARTS

1 IRAQ

A year ago, stuck in a hungry country,
And stung by trouble, by now she had outsung
Beggars with *rababas*. Recently,

Grown thin with a sickness that thickens the tongue,
High in coffee-black nights, she's sworn that she
Would have it split to set it chattering.

2 A HARD PLACE

He says he's had but two thoughts since, and both
Snaky: while one sloughs image after adage,
The other rattles round with tale in mouth.

They'd turn him stone. He'd turn them advantage,
With the grim Greek, who ground a stutter smooth
As gravel rounded in the sea's green rage.

VOICES

Σῶμα, θυμήσου ὄχι μόνο τὸ πόσο ἀγαπήθηκες . . .

In Kolonaki's glassy labyrinth,
At any corner I run into her
And don't. At Zonar's now: an electrolier
Above my table, the gleams of wealthy chatter,
Pier glasses, glossy paneling on each plinth,
Ceiling fans idling. Vitrines of baklava,
Loukoum. "And what if I don't sleep with you?"
We leaned across a table by a mirror,
Maybe this one. As frequently that year,
I had been reading all night in Cavafy
And couldn't see his point, he was so clear.
I read him for the idioms; I read
Him for his rhymes. She bent to kiss her coffee.
Clatter of glass to glass and fork on platter.
The floor in diamonds of marble inlay.
"I'll have to love you, then, forever," she said.
That night it was the perfect thing to say.

PAROS

For James Merrill

1

Hornblasts! They jarred us from the engines' snore
And cheesy air of what the door sign called
The "Dinning Room" to spraydrift, sidechurn. Jade
Clouds on indigo marmalade.
A red line pulled the hooked seasnake, braided,

Slithering, onto shore—where churches sat,
Skyblue-domed (except for one, which wore
A little Byzantine cloche),
Among toy houses, toy hotels.
I slipped the handbooks back into my pack.

I had no notion what I'd come to,
These years ago now. Of course I knew a name.
How often since I've rolled it on my tongue—
Paros, Paros—spoon-sweet of mastic
(Its white a taste of the town's white)

Served in a glass of cold well-water, dissolving,
If at all, more slowly than the sunbow
Airbrushed in spray just off the Leto's bow,
Afterglow of our escort dolphin, now
All these years ago, as we came to.

2

Men on the jetty mending a golden net,
Bacchanalian bougainvillea spilling
Over its trelliswork, swagging plumbago,
And rank lantana, the wayfarer, its flower
Your "little Victorian bouquet"—

33

How many times I've thought the island up—
Its lush aridity, its sundry ravelings.
The stove-in windmill with the winding stair
That someone might restore
Stood near a winepress, overgrown,

And a derelict threshing floor—
Drama itself arrived once more
At its first stages,
Comedy's very threshold being razed . . .
Demeter's temple, built of local marble,

Had long since entered *its* new life:
Stylobate, lintel, drums coursed side by side,
A lucent, clear-cut Doric score of frozen
Music broken and recomposed
Chockablock in the Venetian *kastro,*

Tumbledown now in the heart of town.
We'd come upon it, but we could never *find* it
Back in those streets—or alleys, let's say, that maze
Of sunsplashed whitewash, the candid walkways
Taking us in a new way every day.

3

Plumbago auriculata. Cape plumbago. Formerly thought to cure lead poisoning. Takes poor soil. Needs little water. Leaves drop in heavy frosts but recovery is good. Light blue blossoms may bleach to white. Propagates from cuttings. Slow to start. Stays low without support. Excellent cover. Good background plant. Good filler.
   —*Guide to Mediterranean Gardens*

Pythian the Thasian geometer wrote a letter to Conon in which he asked him how to find a mirror surface such that when it is placed facing the sun the rays reflected from it meet the circumference of a circle. And when Zenodorus the astronomer came down to Arcadia and was introduced to us, he asked us how to find a mirror surface such that when it is placed facing the sun the rays reflected from it meet a point and thus cause burning. So we want to explain the answer to the problem posed by Pythion and to that posed by Zenodorus. . . .

—Diocles, *On Burning Mirrors,* Arabic translation of the lost Greek original, edited with English translation and commentary by G. J. Toomer (with 37 figures and 24 plates)

Tradition has it that Hagia Sophia's master architect dispatched his Parian apprentice, Ignatius, to build a church, at the Emperor Justinian's order, on the site of St. Helena's vision of the True Cross. . . . When the architect visited the island to review the completed structure and found a defect, Ignatius flung himself from the peak. . . . While no such flaw is evident today, it must be admitted that the church's plan is now confused, since, rather like a miniature Canterbury, it has been repeatedly augmented, revised, and restored. (One result is that it is a chasmophile's delight. In addition to the triforium arches, diverse niches, nooks, and alcoves appear as one makes the tour.)

—A. H. Clarendon, *Travels in the Aegean*

4

What was that the dragon kite was writing
In flamboyant Arabic and disappearing ink
There on the high Greek blue sky, its string
In your hands where we stood on a roof's brink
High on the Greek blue sky . . .

I meant to be—yes, a burning mirror!
And yet, back in our cell, with guides, a lexicon,
An old Hachette, what was I "working on"?
Translations? Expenses and itinerary?
And inklings. Linkings . . . Cross-hatching . . .

To church bells' tones, I worried Paros' own
Archilochus' colloquial Ionic,
Bawdy, elegant, and bellicose,
Sharp shards of contumely and elegy—
And bad jokes for his good friend Charilaos.

I knew *to travel* meant *to work*.
I knew whose absence should fill up my pages.
And there it is today: the missing ink.
I wrote: "The strain is telling, in a word."
(The "word" was *telling? strain?* I couldn't think.)

5

A study underway that summer,
High Life Expectancy on the Island of Paros, Greece,
Would postulate some salutary factors:
Scouring winds, rubdowns with olive oil,
Cheese made from milk of goats who graze on thyme.

Also home brews of mint and anise,
Old remedies no one has known to fail,
The occasional miracle, the rarer crime,
The burlap bag beneath the donkey's tail,
Strong local honey, wine, and families.

The antidote for that tattoo of needles,
Sea urchin's spines, snapped off in the heel?
Lean on something and piss on it.
Specific for some sharper pains as well.
Who cared where spring had gone? Or L.

6

And then one evening at the water's edge,
We watched the sunlight's riddle in the shallows,
Wavery cloisonné, a network woven,
Rewoven by the ripples' scission, ply
And reply. Small fish like thoughts shot through and through.

A tied-up rowboat, scarlet, freshly painted,
Glossy as though the lacquer hadn't dried,
Rocked and rocked in light and light reflected.
Some fine idea's fiery cradle.
Flames lapped, waves licked its side.

7

High life indeed. Stylitic penthouse,
The cubicle we'd rented
Was set atop the hotel's second story.
The other rooms had wrought-iron balconies.
We had the roof's wide desert. Beside our entrance,

A crane-necked spigot stood just high enough
To crouch beneath for a chilling shower.
Inside there were two beds, one desk, one chair.
A mirror, a jimmied window. Come cocktail hour,
Our own low roof became a gallery

From which we looked into the open air
Ciné Rex next door. That summer's star
Was Debbie Reynolds as Soeur Sourire,
"The Singing Nun," subtitled in *dimotikí*.
While she strummed her guitar,

You reeled off Apollinaire:
Sous le pont Mirabeau coule la Seine . . .
Water under the bridge. And in our whiskies.
"Here's to Scotching spiteful roomers,"
You could have said. Here's to one loaded paradise,

There *à la belle étoile* . . . *A la belle étoile*:
Phrase from a little carillon. *A la belle*
Etoile. The priest walked through the cloister
At the Church of Our Lady of the Hundred Gates
And pulled on ropes linked hiddenly to bells

Hung in the pine above the lime geraniums,
Whose leaves I crushed and crushed, greedy for the smell,
The sweet reek on my fingers.
We sat beneath the pergola, its star
Jasmine, while bells rang through the white . . . *ruelles*.

8

When the *meltémia* blew
Through and through the bleached streets,
The lanes winding
Beneath pleached vines, winds blue
As Debussy's, they blew disaster out of mind.

After, above the town, on any breeze,
Scent of wild oregano, milder chamomile.
Ah, Mother Demeter.
Our Lady of the Hundred Gates.
The distant hour chiming. Peal and repeal.

9

Beyond the dovecotes, beyond the nunnery,
Up in the grove Dimitri's donkeys plodded to,
Rampant grape and honeysuckle vines
Entwine the trees—arbutus, olive, mulberry,
And two gnarled fig stumps like a pair of Jains.

I see us now. I don't know why we've come
Again until, trading a smile with you,
Dimitri walks through trees, shaking limbs.
From branches where they've lit to rest
On this stage in their long, obscure migration,

Thick as the leaves their closed wings mimic, they spill
And spill, like gusty autumn come back home,
A million vermilion moths, a whole confetti
Of them, as we join in, shaken awake,
Out of the green, out of the blue and still.

HOMECOMING AT LAMMAS

The August sun starts in against the green
And rugged Kansas grain.
The rented Dodge whines on through heat so candid

It puts last year, its palmy days of arak
And cloudy rhetoric,
Flatly in the shade. The very air

Above the pavement wilts, yet feed corn grows
In ranks of tasseled scarecrows
So tall a man could lose his way in it.

The posted fields shoot past, glaring bad rhymes,
Flashing close shaves, cheap rooms,
The shrike's barbed-wire kabob of bug and vole.

Poor, starchy soul, this dry plain seems to say,
Unsoiled habitué
Of souks, casinos, elevating tells,

There are certain states that you must work
Yourself not up but back
Down into. Like the first. Stop here, dig in,

Study the disc, the sprouting stump, cicadas,
And all of those old saws.
Acknowledge the corn: you've been plowing sand.

No root, no fruit. So come on down to earth—
Maybe you'll spring up yet,
Giving as good as you are bound to get.

CARNAL KNOWLEDGE

Now LeRoy on the kill-room floor
Was almost larger than life.
Mondays the green fatigues he wore
Had creases sharp as the knife

That was his very bread and butter,
And his face was hand-carved ebony.
For days the new boy with the stutter
Stayed out of LeRoy's way.

Later that summer he learned to tell
(After LeRoy had his fun)
A skinned pizzle from a skinned tail
And not to grind the one

Into the dogfood mix he'd pour
In boxes, freeze in lots.
He'd scoop up cheeks, as sweet and sour
As rotting apricots,

And fill each barrel till it weighed
Two hundred pounds and more.
The elevator rope had frayed
So many years before

He couldn't look up as he let
His load down twenty feet.
LeRoy laughed to see him sweat
And went on boning meat.

Across the street, at the Blue Moon,
He flashed a friend's draft card
And drank one tall red beer each noon.
The barmaid made it hard

(He would have said he had "a heart on"),
But he'd punch in on time,
Hose the concrete down, then start on
The tripe, slick with chyme.

He marveled at the huge pink lungs
("They's soft as a big gal's knockers")
That he hung up with hearts and tongues
On hooks in chilling lockers.

He learned it paid to be precise.
Learned an esophagus
Was really easier to slice
Than greasy radiator hose.

LeRoy owned he'd eaten dogfood.
The kid swore he would last
Till school began. The pay was good.
"The rules are *hard* and *fast*,"

LeRoy'd sigh. "But they's the *only*
Ones," he'd wink and grin.
"Whatcha do when *you* get lonely?"
Before the days drew in,

He met a girl, wheatshocking blonde.
On weekend nights they drove
Out Sweetbriar Lane and by the pond
Made love, like mad, made love.

INTENSIVE CARE

> I put it to you that this was solely in his sunflower
> state and that his haliodraping het was why maids all
> sighed for him, ventured and vied for him. Hm?
> —*Finnegans Wake*

You might think it could not be done,
Since he'd been strung up so
(Having survived what metamorphosed one
Friend in a flash to what a glossy photo
The D.A. showed him later misconstrued
As some garage sale mannequin,
The other to a jailbird, denim blue),

And cast in plaster from the chest
Down to one heel, to boot.
You might think that, disabled, he'd at last
Be able to button up, to imitate,
If ever, the Saint who stood out like a statute
Beyond the frosted panes and blessed
The molded pigeons and the molting too.

You might . . . Yet under snowpacked nurses'
Suspicious noses, in spite
Of Demerol, in spite of tranquilizers,
Pulleys and wires, they made him almost nightly
(God love their never-say-die attitude)
See how it could be even worse,
That accident that he kept coming through.

THE RACKET

For Elizabeth Bramblett Yenser

Although the numbers all have dropped away
Tonight, above the hospital, insensibly,

Coldly the stars insist on the old rite:
They hang around demanding their connections.

Some are ancient, well-fixed enough to need
Hardly a glance. And some are even dead.

Those are the silent partners in the racket,
Crackling network of systems, tracks, concessions,

Contracts effected by long-distance calls,
Addiction fed by any vice at all.

It's shadier than night itself, shameless.
And yet, in truth, in light of shafts so spindly,

How in the world is that unearthly darkness
Ever to be born

Up under, if not by plots, shots in the dark,
And whole fan vaults of tracers, traceries . . .

Now the moon, too, her own unlucky number
Nearly up, though losing face,

Complexion gone, and figure gone to boot,
Has come around, pathetically expectant.

But nothing's new beneath the moon. *Mundus
Alter et idem*, Mother. Moondust

Settles on old scores, ledgers, calla lilies.
While high up in a corner of the window

Another web's begun
To hang there like the Hunter, or the Scales

To which with each long shot, with each leased breath
We're being drawn, in which we will be weighed.

A TABLE OF GREENE FIELDS

For Willard Yenser

Your wife, who polished verse,
Was duty-bound to quarrel
With much that we'd rehearse
For you at the corner billiard parlor:
The homespun language,
And where to put the accents
For English and massé,
And how to break loose racks,

And cut, and kiss, and bridge.
You never could insist
That we play for small change
But hated to see us risk
Minimum wages
Before we'd learned to hold
Our own with hustlers
Whom you'd have shot blindfold.

Now, shuffling through a haze
Denser than that in Scotty's
Those hot, long Saturdays
You worry you've forgotten
There by your river, where duller
Colors carom from bank
To bank across
The fading felt, the rankest

Double-cross, you play
Again. You're under the gun
Again and bound to stay,
As always, till you've won—
Or followed through
On one last stroke and seen
That the sun has spun
Home under darkening green.

III

VERTUMNAL

Close *call*, close *call*, close *call*: this early in the morning
The raucous crows' raw caws are ricochets off rock.

Afloat on wire from a dead tree's branch a piece of charred limb
Repeats a finch that perched on it in its last life.

Here under the pergola, loaded with green wistaria,
Misty air wistful with a few late lavender clusters,

Light falling in petal-sized spots across the notebook page
(Falling just now for instance on the phrase *Light falling*),

And under the feeder where the thumb-sized Calliope hummer
Hovers like a promising word on wings thrumming

To slip her bill-straw past the busy sugar ants
Through the red flower's grill into the sweetened red water,

And over there in your "office" under the lean-to under the crabapple,
Its fruit (like tiny ottomans) rotting sweetly on the branch

(Bouquet of Calvados and fresh tobacco),
Where in the midst of spades and pruners, hatchets, hoes, and shears,

Trowels, dibbles, rakes, and sickles you ground your axes,
Sharpened your wits, filed your notes and journals,

Moving through the garden, through all you made of where you lived—
You catch your ex-son-in-law, taking photos, figs, and notes on notes.

2

All round the garden are ghosts of what we called your "sculptures":
Pruned limbs, and broken, dried out to dove-gray, steel-gray,

Balanced, cantilevered, interlocked like skeletons
Of lovers, wrestlers, lovers; dried vines dangling

From a high branch and snaking up a makeshift bench;
A lonely felloe with its Vs of spokes against a wall;

A lithe gnarl of live oak, grain rainwashed,
Sundrawn into shape, head cocked, curious,

Wedged in its hanging basket—as though in some square nest?
Whimsical, estranged, you left it all up in the air.

The ancient plum tree, its chief remaining limb become its trunk,
Leans on a forked crutch stuck in earth.

Disfigured, splendid in its beads of resin,
It has been dying twenty years. *Go slow,* you'd say,

On any occasion of stress or lift: *Go slow*—
Unhurried as the date palm, your family around you nervous as finches.

Weeding, staking, mulching, always with some startled kerchief
Or boxers remnant or paisley necktie binding your brow.

Things ripened. Rounded out. Entered new lives by smidgins.
By pulses. You went slow. And suddenly were gone.

3

Brassily proud of your descent, you still had little Polish—
And less polish. You read no poetry yet wrote a lot—

Sometimes reinventing Cavafy in the rough
("We need not forget the love that was not bestowed").

Newmanian from nose to mottoes ("Growth proves life"),
Catholic existentialist, you thought all others,

Abbagnano through Zubiri, alien kindred souls—
Born thin, pedestrian, worn through—or kindred heels.

Belligerent as Pound in his egregious master-baiting,
You scoffed at "experts," believed in nature's living art,

Like the piece of driftwood that, when stood on end,
Changed to a naked figure poised *en pointe,* a rib scooped out,

Yet couldn't leave unchanged whatever came your way.
Pie tins flashed in the olive and the fig—not to scare birds,

Either, but to catch the sun—and catch the moon.
You would have fixed the Adam on a pedestal . . . So I did.

No one would put you there. Nor were you in paradise
Alone, although you loved to be alone. And maybe now you are—

Alone with your thoughts, with galaxies, with nebulae
Slowly exploding forever behind your peerless, newly opened eyes.

4

You cut the thorny lemon, and it cut back. Your fingers,
Cross-hatched, were thick as roots, with eyes of their own,

In queer places, like potatoes' eyes, and noses of their own,
Used as moles to breaking earth—

Densely wrinkled, blunt, penile. Well, Raymond V. Bomba,
The V for Valentine, whose day you were born on, we miss you,

Old Vertumnus. The V for *verto* and all its furcations.
And for the Virgin in the birdbath's center in the garden's

Who sees you still, the blanket hung to screen a rift in greenery,
Taking your sunbath—hunkered naked, or standing naked, a little bent.

V for the forked wand and "the poor bare forked animal."
Sorting your "effects," your wife and daughter found a clutch

Of photos clipped and cropped and pasted into thoughtful paginal
Compositions or left loose to be shuffled. A fingered muff

Matches a bearded mouth, a pinkish cock and a stiff tongue rhyme.
The edges have been tenderly rounded. (For once you cut some corners.)

Hankering, reverent, you left them there to tell the family—what?
There in the old goat shed across from guava and kumquat . . .

Kumquat. Who would not succumb to the word, its verjuice
And blown kiss? V also for all that's venial, vernacular.

In the new *Romance Philology,* a title you'd have savored:
"Vegetal-Genital Onomastics in the *Libro de Buen Amor.*"

Wonderful mouthful, its palatals, its labials!
V for its *g*'s as soft as August's livid purple figs,

So swollen in the fondling sun they have a frosty glaze.
Under the fig tree, an old pot's full of drying *cardone,*

Pappus coarse as pubic hair, with a fresh, fierce pungency,
Burst buds gone oily brown, starseeds forming in death.

Ray, you could have told us that the same root shoots
Its milky sap through *work* and *orgy* too.

You dug pits for your rakings, grounds, rinds,
Wormy peppers, tomatoes simmered on the summer vines,

And apricots galore—windfallen, slug-gnawed, earwig-bored,
Daintily painted with snailglister and bird droppings,

Or chucked by squirrels who'd take a cheeky bite
From just-ripe fruit and drop the ruin at your feet.

Fruit ripe and rife, fire-dipped, as the poet put it,
And proved upon the earth. And it is still a law

That all goes in, serpentine, vatic, dreaming on the hills—
Lavender, vespid, vibrant—this evening's hills of heaven.

Propped on a bench against a squatting, warty stump,
A fragment of a dealer's license frame says SANTA MONICA.

Your kind of icon. Though in the Texas house you grew up in,
And kept, and opened once a year, near Beeville, where you were born,

Every surface has its Sacred Heart or crucifix,
Its holy card, or palm branch blessed with holy water, or string of bead

One rosary seemed so old I rolled and warmed it in my hands
Then smelled to see if it were made indeed of crushed rose petals.

We broomed the cobwebs from the smokeshed and the washshed
And knocked the wasps' nests down from behind the jalousies.

I hacked dewberries that held the footing in a barbed embrace
And planed and sanded swollen doors so they would close.

They would not close. "We have slown down," your daughter,
Sundumb, mumbled truly—and we could hardly fasten up,

Evenings, as we lolled and mulled in that salty latitude,
That intense lassitude, mugged by the wet heat,

Longing's very weather. On your screened porch we chewed
On local sayings, spit and scratched, and stewed in our own juices.

The old Norge plugged away beside the chair where you once read.
"The dead sing out," you'd scribbled, "for are we not the dead?"

A pair of wild parrots startle
Up overhead and squabble off together wholeheartedly.

Here where your family had their gin and tonic talks,
And I took issue and drinks with twists on mazy walks,

African lindens flourish—exactly where I wed your daughter.
Coaxing them from cuttings, I didn't see that she lacked sun and water.

The year turned round each year with canteloupe and plum,
Eggplant and olive, and the vowel-dark grapes of autumn

Tied to the arbor. And as it happens, the ball of twine
Has just run out you gave to us with our first vine . . .

So where am I? *Twine* . . . Mona's word, who gave us tarragon—
And gave us too, too late, a poem . . . Its purple aura gone

To ground around it, a *pointilliste*'s shadow, mystical,
The jacaranda dangles pods like desiccated testicles.

The grackle, the early bird—"the *oily* one"—will get the worm
Even as it turns. The marriage went full term,

Went unpicked, then fell like you. *Marriage,* from *mari,*
Young woman, bride . . . *tried* . . . *tied* . . . as *though* to *mara,*

Bitter. The olive's argentine, then argen*tine. Twine, twine* . . .
Terms mean, demean . . . Ray, you'd cure the bitter fruit in brine.

one night a dark light shone   moon like a thinning dime   some Ro-
man figure   mercurial   face dimmed with radiance   out in the
garden the lemon tree's own dark bulbs shown by it showed me a way
among your labyrinthine plots of greens   on this land scorning profits
you cultivated kale and cabbage   well flesh is grass and things are
fire the obscure Greek claims as goods are gold   while money too as
someone puts it is just a kind of poetry   I think you'd think he meant
it's always passing on   clinking to link like charms its users up from
A to Z   or does *it* use *us* up (grown shiny and wrinkled) in its
rounds   now you were passing on were you a kind of poetry   a sheaf
of notes   snap a bill or rap a half dollar on the counter and speak
the magic formula (*change please!*) and it turns into something else
eerie   *tink-tink* of wind chimes   a hint of mint beside the molded
Virgin   shoulders rounded as the shepherd's   lambent   the green
the fluent moon dough   quarters are given   taken   given and
taken   but first they're coined   like phrases   I hope you'll see
your own way clear to these   Ray   who were (once clouds had
gathered) their solitary shaft of light

9

You'd "made a living" joining sounds with images—
Like the crystalline *blps* with stones thrown in the freshet

In *The Sound of Music.* Following the clever songs you spliced
("*Do*—a female deer, *re*—a drop of golden sun, *mi* . . . "),

The Trapps escaped—while you walked off unnoticed with a Golden
      Reel.
And you escaped from Fox, but not before you'd paid, with *Patton,*

With hearing failing you like headphones in *The French Connection.*
Invasions, traps that you could not evade awaited

You in your ultramontane garden, beyond the Hollywood Hills,
Where the Reel itself would serve some realer purpose.

(Its base, engraved, sat on a low bookshelf, humiliated.)
After cocktails you'd shamble down to lock the gate behind us.

Through the car window, I'd clasp your rough glove of a hand.
We'd leave you where the twilit freeway's soft white noise

Was the golden rule. Where I'd first pressed your daughter's hand.
I've sometimes thought if you had lived I'd not have let it go.

But then we must let go. It was almost as though I died
To her when you did, and as though it were you I couldn't leave—

As though somehow you'd been my father too.
As though at last without you anything were possible to do.

We cannot know, and yet I know you started to leave life
The way I'd later take the plane from Los Cabos:

One wasn't eager but had had enough of the guacamole
And your beloved mariachi to have standards set forever after.

Now and again the snorkeling had been breathtaking,
That life below life, the flit of selflit fish in sunken cities,

Although one had been banged by this wave or that,
Into a rocky pocket at the reef's tip, and socked about,

Yet escaped, but bruised and cut, if punctually, cheaply stitched.
I think your soul had begun to hover over our quick, hungry lives

The way the scuba diver hovers over busy schools,
The way the parasailor aspires to utter silence above white beach

Where horses dream a canter up and drifts with scissortails
Above The Two Heads, The Bishop, toward The Point,

Where Ocean marries Sea, once and for all, day after day—
Beyond the two sides of The Beach of Love,

One on the Sea, the other steps away on the so-called Pacific,
Which is not, which is cold, and turbulent, and *Muy Peligroso*.

At picnic's end, at land's, the day comes down to ice cubes on the sand,
Netted in the spume, sparkling whole seconds in the setting sun.

II

A squeaking cupboard—no, the hummingbird, eking out a song,
Looking it might be for material for his nest, a matrix

Woven of hair, saliva threads, plant down, spider web, and lichen,
Lichen itself already complex, alga, fungus . . .

You tried to weave it all together too—in verse, in prose—
And get it straight as well. But how could you compose

In *stanzas,* who wrote among the ferns, and feverfew in flower,
Where fennel alone could hold elaborate candelabra up?

And what could you have had to do with *argument,*
Who hardly threw a thing away and even made blue plastic

Bottle caps, immortal rubbish, seem to grow on trees?
"Beyond Words" you entitled the last draft

Of your ever denser, ever more desperate manuscript.
Beyond palaver, you meant, and academic poppycock,

Folderal and flourish, terms that squelch and fix—
Like chokeberry corymbs and spikes of heather.

And chickweed cyme, jack-in-the-pulpit's spadix,
And the calla lily's, milkweed umbel,

Panicle of wild oat grass, thyrse of lilac . . .
All that malarkey, flashy as the Texas meadowlark's.

The house you built will go, wall by wall, to Encinada's sand.
Your garden will give way to filters, pumps, floodlights.

Where will the squirrels go to stir up their old quarrels?
Where will the gopher go, who loves a life among fig roots?

This early morning's mockingbird's a rusty screw
Coming out a half turn at a time.

With such an effort you'd twist your thoughts free.
Or on your Adler bang them deeper into mystery.

Trying to write your hard time down,
You found time writing you down first, with your own pencils,

Always growing stubbier, shavings fragrant as cumin,
Fragrant as made love, erasing their own erasers.

How you loathed "realities sustained too long—
As with the saint, who can't do anything but pray . . .

Are we not always part of something else
That also needs to live, to die, to change?"

—That from your journals with their words of orchards,
Orchards of words, their round redundance, while the breeze

Sweeps the albizzia, its easy dance redone of light and shade,
Beside the wild firetop that's suddenly abuzz with bees.

MOVING AGAIN

In memoriam Howard Nemerov (1920–1991)

1

So that's your level best,
Stretching behind like the Forsaken Plain.

Not much, it flatly says, and then:
There's no time like the present to leave,
Unless it is the past.

And what is there in such an evening
To take advantage of? What pools or seas
To look into like—like possibilities?

The entrails that you might inspect
Turn out to be the same wry paths
Giving their opposite directions.

So still you're hardly moved, although
You do not know, precisely, where
They go.

2

To routes that ramify
Forever, like cryptic roots, so you've imagined,

Or straight down into long box canyons
In petrifying foothills
Slow-motioned down through centuries to lie

Rugose as elephants,
Or up by ways just as inscrutable
To the graveyard of white elephants,

Alkaline valleys and ravines
Shadowed indelibly by that berseem
Which like desire will spring up anywhere,

And higher yet, up to the lake
Which seems to wear the glazed and fragile look
Of some beginning's thinnest ice.

3

But just now, for the briefest
Space, there's nothing there to face,

Like the first pyramid the night
It held its piece
Out of the growing puzzle of the stars

Only to come to hand
This night, almost the door ajar
Of the next house you'll have to find,

Through which you'll have to move,
And which in one way or another
Or both at once for once

And all will have to level
With you, becoming then the last
Imperfect undertaking left behind.